A QUESTION OF SUCCESSION

OTHER BOOKS BY ALEX MITCHELL

Quizzin' Nine-Nine: A Brooklyn Nine-Nine Quiz Book
Parks & Interrogation: A Parks & Recreation Quiz Book
Q & AC-12: A Line of Duty Quiz Book
Know Your Schitt: A Schitt's Creek Quiz Book
Examilton: A Hamilton Quiz Book
Stranger Thinks: A Stranger Things Quiz Book
The El Clued Brothers: A Peep Show Quiz Book
Dunder Quizlin: An Office US Quiz Book

A Question of Succession

A *Succession* Quiz Book

Published by Beartown Press

Copyright © 2020 Alex Mitchell

This book is unofficial, unauthorized and in no way associated with the *Succession* television production. Please don't set the Roy family lawyers on me.

ISBN: 9798694157643

For Greg.

The world's tallest dwarf.

The weakest strong man at the circus.

And the poorest rich person in America.

Contents

Introduction	11
General Knowledge	13
General Knowledge	15
General Knowledge	17
General Knowledge	19
General Knowledge	21
General Knowledge	23
General Knowledge	25
Logan	27
Kendall	28
Shiv	30
Roman	32
Connor	34
Tom	36
Greg	38
Marcia	40
Gerri	42
Insults	44
Complete the Quote	45
Connor's Heartfelt Eulogy	47
Complete the Quote	48
Who Am I?	50
Anagrams	52
Who Said It?	53

In Real Life	55
Kendall's Rap	57
Cast & Crew	59
Tiebreakers	60
ANSWERS	63

Introduction

Succession has all the ingredients you want in a business-focused comedy-drama. Dysfunctional family? Check. Underhand boardroom shenanigans? Check. Weaponized dialogue? Check.

In Logan, Kendall, Shiv, Roman, Connor, Tom, Greg et all, it has a perfectly-crafted core of characters who deliver that rare, *Friends*-like quality of allowing you to recognize the person from reading the line alone. (See the 'Who Said It?' round for proof of this.)

As a disillusioned office worker myself, I've also found *Succession* to be an extremely useful source of corporate etiquette and boardroom buzz phrases. By 2022 I expect to have either smashed the glass ceiling or be preparing to face an industrial tribunal.

Anyway, in a nutshell, what have on your hands here are 27 themed rounds of questions all about *Succession*, including a set of tiebreakers to separate the Yaystars from the Naystars.

If you're not totally up-to-date on *Succession*, please be aware that this book contains spoilers (obviously).

But now, if you're ready to prove you're a worthy successor to the Roy crown, let's get started...

General Knowledge

1. Which sport do the Roys play in the opening episode?

2. Who does Logan trick into signing the papers that will confirm Marcia as his successor?

3. Tom's birthday gift to Logan is quickly regifted to somebody else. Who?

4. What medical condition is Logan struck by at the close of episode one?

5. Who gives Shiv $20 to buy sodas at the hospital?

6. Who is the youngest of Logan's children?

7. What subject does Tom note is absent from the prenuptial agreement drawn up by Shiv?

8. What role does Roman rejoin the company in?

9. Who does Roman spend most of his first days back at the company with?

10. Who does a frustrated Shiv hire to conduct a background check on Marcia?

Answers on page 65

General Knowledge

1. At which event does Logan announce his return to running the company?

2. Who tips Logan off about Kendall's speech after noticing the prompter text?

3. During their final handover, Bill Lockheart informs Tom of the company's cover-up of crimes committed where?

4. Who joins the board as a result of Kendall's deal to protect the company's share price?

5. What is Willa's former profession?

6. Greg drives Ewan 12 hours to the rest of the Roys for which occasion?

7. Which items does Logan show to Willa?

8. Leading up to the vote of no confidence, Greg has two dinners in the same night. Who are they with?

9. Why is the president apparently unable to meet with Logan?

10. What does Logan say is the only reason Ewan joined the Vietnam War?

Answers on page 66

General Knowledge

1. Which two people abstain from voting, in the vote of no confidence?

2. At the vote of no confidence, which four board members vote against Logan?

3. Who plants the news stories about Kendall's drug use?

4. Which project is Roman put in charge of overseeing?

5. Who hosts the weekend-long therapy session at their own place?

6. Who does Logan ask to keep an eye on Kendall during Tom's bachelor party?

7. Kendall and Frank meet two young entrepreneurs looking for angel investment into their business, which is what?

8. To which city did the bachelor party attendees believe they would be going?

9. In what building does it actually take place?

10. Roman switched the location expressly to meet with which business magnate?

Answers on page 67

General Knowledge

1. Who altruistically does Kendall's last two lines of cocaine at Tom's bachelor party?

2. Who was annoyed at not going to Prague for the bachelor party, as he'd been setting up his circadian rhythm for two weeks?

3. Which subject is Connor "on the verge of" starting a podcast on?

4. What is the name of Kendall, Shiv and Roman's mother?

5. Which job does Connor decide he wants, while at Shiv's wedding?

6. Who does Tom kick out of the wedding (and return the wine they'd just poured back to the bottle)?

7. What is the name of the young waiter who dies in the car accident with Kendall?

8. Roman begins dating Tabitha. Which other member of the family has she had a (brief) romantic encounter with?

9. Where do the Roys arrive for a family break in the first episode of season two?

10. What is the stench in the family cottage?

Answers on page 68

General Knowledge

1. While Logan is gently welcoming Kendall back into the fold, Shiv reminds him that he once beat Roman with a slipper for ordering... what?

2. What is Kendall's reason for shutting down Lawrence's company?

3. Apart from himself, can you name either of the two individuals Logan wanted Shiv to shadow as part of her preparation for the role of Waystar CEO?

4. Who wants to digitize the TV media company in order to drive efficiencies?

5. Who is brought back into the Waystar fold due to their relationship with Nan Pierce?

6. In which country does the company retreat take place?

7. Which animals do the Roys go hunting for there?

8. What is the name of the hazing "game" Logan subjects his potentially traitorous employees to?

9. What is the charming name of the background-checker hired to find out if someone in the inner circle has spoken to Michelle Pantsil?

10. What is Moe's real first name, as Willa learns shortly after greeting his grieving widow?

Answers on page 69

General Knowledge

1. What type of animal is Roman dressed as during his management training?

2. Who was Mark Ravenhead's dog named after?

3. What was the original quote Tom and Greg planned to give to address public outcry over the emerging cruise scandal?

4. Who is convinced to send someone a naked picture of themselves?

5. What is written on the envelope in which Greg was storing the incriminating copies of the cruise documents?

6. What type of pie does Caroline serve to Kendall, Roman and Shiv?

7. Name either of the two demands Caroline offers Logan the choice of in exchange for her shareholder support?

8. What is Logan's mother's name?

9. What proportion of Willa's play's dialogue is unfinished?

10. What is the name of the lead actress in the play, who Kendall charms away?

Answers on page 70

General Knowledge

1. What jersey number is Kendall wearing during his rap performance?

2. "NRPI" is the justification for the cruise line coverup. What does it stand for?

3. Who claims not to know Greg during the proceedings before Congress?

4. Which two Waystar employees are taken hostage along with Roman?

5. What is the name of the man Roman manages to broker a verbal financing agreement with during the hostage situation?

6. Who manages to convince the assault victim to take the money, rather than testifying?

7. Who offers themselves up as the "blood sacrifice", before being turned down?

8. Who does Kendall suggest is "theoretically perfect" for the sacrifice?

9. Who is the common denominator in all of Roman's suggestions for the sacrifice?

10. What is the name of the DJ who drops a beat for Kendall?

Answers on page 71

Logan

1. Which birthday is Logan "celebrating" in the first episode?

2. In which city was Logan born?

3. Where is Logan when he suffers his stroke?

4. Whose office does Logan relieve himself in?

5. Who does Logan slap with a jar of Cranberry sauce at Thanksgiving?

6. What was the name of Logan's sister?

7. What is the name of the college Logan is funding?

8. What was the purpose of the loan Logan took out for the company, which was secured against the Waystar stock price?

9. Which football club does Logan support?

10. What is Logan's condition for investing in Willa's play?

Answers on page 72

Kendall

1. What is the name of Kendall's ex-wife?

2. What is his son's name?

3. How many children does Kendall have?

4. How much money does Sandy Furness offer Kendall for his stake in Waystar Royco?

5. Which university did Kendall and Stewy attend together?

6. In which country did Kendall's rehab take place, between seasons one and two?

7. What is the first item we see Kendall shoplift?

8. Who else is in the helicopter when Kendall (briefly) almost takes off in it while high?

9. Which word does Kendall chastise Jennifer for using twice during her brief introduction to Logan?

10. Who flies with Kendall to New York ahead of the press conference at which he is expected to take the fall for the cruise line scandal?

Answers on page 73

Shiv

1. With whom does Shiv have a physical fight in the first episode of *Succession*?

2. Which aspiring presidential candidate did Shiv represent before abruptly departing her role?

3. Which role within his team does that presidential candidate promote Shiv to?

4. Shiv springs into damage control mode when a political client accidentally posts a particular photo on social media. What does the photo show?

5. Who was going to give Shiv away at her wedding, in Logan's absence?

6. Shiv accidentally insults Mark Pierce when she jokes about his PhD saving him 12 seconds on which website?

7. When Tom is trying to select a present for Logan, within what value range does Shiv advise Tom to make sure it looks like?

8. What is the name of the venue in which Shiv gets married?

9. Rhea approaches Shiv with a job offer. What is the role?

10. What item does Shiv gift to her father at his fiftieth anniversary gala?

Answers on page 74

Roman

1. In the first episode, Roman offers a kid $1m if he can do what?

2. What is Roman's actual first name?

3. What does Roman claim Kendall, Connor and Shiv forced him to eat at four years old?

4. Which event did Roman bring forward the satellite launch to coincide with?

5. Which role does Roman take at Waystar Royco in season one?

6. In which country is Roman held hostage in season two?

7. Who knocks out Roman's tooth during season two?

8. Which soccer club does Roman (incorrectly) buy for his father as a gift?

9. What is the name of the girlfriend Roman meets at Tom's bachelor party?

10. How long is the Waystar Royco management course Roman begins in season two?

Answers on page 75

Connor

1. What does Connor gift to Logan for his birthday in the first episode?

2. What is the name of Willa's play, which Connor convinces Logan to invest in?

3. What does Connor intend to get rid of when he becomes president?

4. What is the name of Connor's New Mexico ranch, where the family therapy session takes place?

5. What is the only statement Connor will allow the journalist to publish about him in "her little book"?

6. How much did Connor pay a guy in a bar to take his terminally-ill dog and give it a good life?

7. Which famous appendage did Connor apparently buy for $500k in season two?

8. Where does Roman claim that Connor "literally only knows about [jail] from"?

9. What does Connor believe is one day going to be "more precious than gold"?

10. What is Connor's message to his father in the video montage for his fiftieth anniversary with the company?

Answers on page 76

Tom

1. What birthday gift does Tom give to Logan in the opening episode?

2. What is Tom's surname?

3. Which state is Tom from?

4. Who wants a "business open relationship" with Tom?

5. What was the subject line of the email Tom sent to Greg 67 times in one evening?

6. Who plans Tom's bachelor party?

7. Which job does Shiv convince Logan to promote Tom to during season two?

8. What does Tom eat off Logan's plate while confronting him on the yacht?

9. What does Tom pretend to take a call about to extricate himself and Shiv during dinner with the Pierces?

10. From whom does Tom inherit both a job title and knowledge of the cruise ship scandals?

Answers on page 77

Greg

1. What is Greg's surname?

2. What animal is Greg dressed at while vomiting through the eyes of his Waystar Royco costume in the first episode?

3. According to Caroline, what was Greg's childhood nickname?

4. What does Greg request that he be called, rather than Greg?

5. What does Tom suggest would be "a great title for [Greg's] memoir"?

6. In the final episode of season two, Tom makes fun of Greg for having a favorite... what?

7. Who allows Greg to live in their apartment, while it waits to be rented out?

8. What is the value of the inheritance Greg will lose out on if he defies his grandfather's orders to quit Waystar Royco?

9. Who does Greg believe he might have touched at the conference for billionaires?

10. From which affliction does Greg suffer, impeding his adherence to the dress code aboard the family yacht?

Answers on page 78

Marcia

1. In which country was Marcia born?

2. Who has a background check carried out on Marcia in season one?

3. What task does Marcia invite Logan to do for himself, while he is struggling with his rehabilitation?

4. What is Marcia's son called?

5. In which European city did Marcia live before moving to America?

6. What was Marcia's job before she married her first husband?

7. What does Marcia task Greg with retrieving from the house, to get him out of the way?

8. Of whom does Marcia enquire if they are regularly tested for sexually transmitted diseases?

9. Who does Marcia invite to Thanksgiving without Logan's knowledge?

10. True or false: Marcia has more lines across season one and season two than Willa?

Answers on page 79

Gerri

1. What is Gerri's surname?

2. What is her job title at Waystar Royco?

3. What is the name of Gerri's former husband?

4. How many years ago does Gerri tell Kendall she and Frank first came to the castle at which Shiv and Tom's wedding takes place?

5. Gerri visits a hospital with Roman in season two. In which country is it?

6. Who is Gerri godmother to?

7. After Kendall is agreed as temporary CEO, Gerri reveals to him that the company is in debt by what figure?

8. Which role does Gerri turn down in the aftermath of Logan's admission to hospital?

9. Complete the term by which Gerri refers to Roman: "You little _____ puppy."

10. True or false: Gerri has more lines across season one and season two than Connor does?

Answers on page 80

Insults

Can you name the *Succession* character by another character's insulting description of them?

1. "An unshaven candle."

2. "A competent kind of clever filing cabinet."

3. "Like a sex robot for Dad to f*ck."

4. "Kim Jong Pop."

5. "Calamari c*ck-ring."

6. "Dildo dipped in beard trimmings."

7. "Little Machiavellian f*ck."

8. "Honey badger."

9. "The c*nt of Monte Cristo."

10. "F*cking Californian shrunken little raisin."

Answers on page 81

Complete the Quote

1. "Gerri, excuse me, but I've always thought of you - and I mean this in the best possible way - as a _____-_____ _____ _____." - Roman.

2. "The _____ is too cold! The _____'s all f*cked! You're f*ckwads and you f*cked it!" - Connor.

3. "Greg sprinkles are a fantastic _____ to absolutely anyone seated at this table." - Roman.

4. "Yeah, we're fine. I've had worse experiences. I once stayed at a _____." - Roman.

5. "What I think he meant to say was that he wished that Mom gave birth to a _____ _____, because at least then it would be useful." - Roman.

6. "But you know, in the end, it's up to you, kiddo. Mmm? Uncle Fun or _____ _____." - Logan.

7. "[Logan] didn't apologize when he hit our au pair with his car. It was her fault for _____ _____ _____, he said." - Roman.

8. "I'm the patsy! I'm the meat in the sandwich. Gerri is the _____ _____." - Tom.

9. "I am interested in becoming a _____ _____." - Kendall.

10. "This was supposed to be choreographed. That's about as choreographed as a _____ getting _____ on _____ _____." - Logan.

Answers on page 82

Connor's Heartfelt Eulogy

Can you name the missing words in Connor's emotionally-charged eulogy for Lester?

"I am here as a fellow (1)_____ to acknowledge that Lester has, as we know, passed on. Lester was a (2)_____. Also Lester was an (3)_____ of the Waystar company for (4)_____ years. And when a man dies, it is (5)_____. All of us will die someday. In this case, it is Lester who has done so. Lester was alive for (6)_____ years, but no more. Now he is dead. Lester's (7)_____ is (8)_____. They were married for (9)_____ years. Now she is (10)_____."

Answers on page 83

Complete the Quote

1. "If I was to give Tom a letter grade, I'd give him a B+ for _____ _____ _____." - Frank.

2. "This is great. You're not going to ruin a party over a couple of fucking _____." - Roman.

3. "Romulus, when you laugh, please do it in the same volume as everyone else. We didn't get you from a _____ _____." - Logan.

4. "Wherever you hide, the _____ finds you." - Greg.

5. "What is that [fragrance] – _____ _____ by Calvin Klein?" - Shiv.

6. "You know who drinks milk? _____ and _____." - Roman.

7. "I'm not declining, I'm just not _____." - Shiv.

8. "Is there an angle here for a team-up? Like me, kind of like a Jagger/Tarzan fronting things up [...] and you back home cooking us soup and making sure the numbers are right. Hmm? _____ and the _____ _____?" - Roman.

9. "[Being rich] is like being a superhero, only better. You get to do what you want. The authorities can't really touch you. You get to wear a costume, but it's designed by _____." - Tom.

10. "You know, Waystar? Waystar Royco. We do _____ _____ and rollercoasters." - Roman.

Answers on page 84

Who Am I?

1. According to Roman, I could be the perfect little cherry on top of a Tom sundae.

2. I'm what it looks like when you resolve all your issues.

3. I sort of cheated on my partner but not really, because all of my fluids stayed in my own body, like a closed loop system.

4. I'm Logan's second wife, and I like to ask people at weddings how long they think the marriage will last.

5. Unfortunately I'm not a big enough fish.

6. I generally only eat Pulitzer.

7. I want a f*cking onion to taste like a peach. I also blackmailed my own son.

8. I'm disappointed that we got construction sand instead of desert sand.

9. I may have Shanghai'd my new husband into an open-borders free-f*ck trade deal on our wedding day, but I still have the greatest hair on television.

10. My dad isn't sure that I'm a killer.

Answers on page 85

Anagrams

Can you unscramble the names of these characters?

1. Brainy Oohs?

2. Canine Rep?

3. Darkly Lone?

4. Mambo Twangs?

5. Loan Orgy?

6. Corny Or No?

7. Hoggish Cryerr?

8. Milk Enlarger?

9. No Armory?

10. A Minor Piece?

Answers on page 86

Who Said It?

Who delivered these classic *Succession* lines?

1. "I saw their plan, and my dad's was better."

2. "I'm dumb but I'm smart."

3. "I have fought and I have lost, and I have fought and won, but when I lose, the other one will generally lose an eye or so."

4. "Oh, uh, yeah. I think I know one [member of Congress]. Representative Ferdinand D. Who Gives a S**t from the great state of No One F**king Cares."

5. "You don't hear much about syphilis these days. Very much the MySpace of STDs."

6. "You know my friend from Paris who was your way? She was actually murdered. It was nothing to do with her being a prostitute, it was to do with a restaurant that went poof!"

7. "The next Zucker f*cker comes along and swallows you whole, sh*ts you out as an app."

8. "Sometimes I think I'll never truly understand dad until I sh*t outside."

9. "Do I go Hulk, or Bruce Banner?"

10. "Hey, uh, big fan of, uh, all your money."

Answers on page 87

In Real Life

1. Which comedy actor and Saturday Night Live alumnus is an executive producer for the show?

2. Who is the youngest of the actors who play Logan's children?

3. Which Guy Ritchie movie does Jeremy Strong appear in with Matthew McConaughey?

4. What does the J in J. Smith Cameron's name stand for?

5. Until Brian Cox suggested it, Logan wasn't going to be Scottish. Where was he originally planned to be from?

6. Which 1994 Keanu Reeves action movie does Alan Ruck appear in?

7. Kieran Culkin appeared in the *Home Alone* movies with his brother Macauley, but what was Kieran's character's name?

8. Which famous Jane Austen character has Matthew Macfadyen played?

9. Which member of the cast has won an Oscar?

10. What nationality is Sarah Snook?

Answers on page 88

Kendall's Rap

Can you fill in the missing words in Kendall's rap to Logan?

"Born on the (1)_____ _____

King of the East Side

Fifty years strong, now he's rollin' in a (2)_____ _____

Handmade suits

Raking in (3)_____

Five-star general, y'all best salute, yo

Bitches be catty

But the king's my daddy

Rock all the haters while we go roll a (4)_____

Squiggle on the decks

Kenny on the rhymes

And Logan big ballin' on (5)_____ _____."

"L to the OG

Dude be the OG

A-N he playin'

Playin' like a pro, see

L to the OG

Dude be the OG

A-N he playin'

Playin' like a pro."

"A1 ratings, 80K (6)_____

Never gonna stop, baby, f*ck (7)_____ _____, bro

Don't get it twisted

I've been through hell

But since I (8)_____ dad, I'm alive and well

Shaper of views

Creator of (9)_____

Father of many, paid all his dues

So don't try to run

Your mouth at the king

Just pucker up, bitch, and go kiss the (10)_____."

Answers on page 89

Cast & Crew

1. Who created the show?

2. Who plays Logan?

3. Who plays Shiv?

4. Who plays Tom?

5. Who plays Kendall?

6. Who plays Roman?

7. Who directed the first episode of *Succession*?

8. Who plays Greg?

9. Who plays Connor?

10. Who plays Gerri?

Answers on page 90

Tiebreakers

1. In which year did *Succession* first air?

2. What does the Waystar Royco share price fall below to trigger the bank's full repayment clause in the loan agreement?

3. What percentage of Waystar Royco does Logan's second wife Caroline own?

4. How much does Logan invest in Willa's play?

5. According to Connor when he's talking to Greg, what amount of money is "a nightmare"?

6. How tall is Greg?

7. How many Primetime Emmy Awards did *Succession* win at the 2020 ceremony?

8. In real life, how many years older is Brian Cox (Logan) than his on-screen son Alan Ruck (Connor)?

9. What amount of time passes between the end of season one and the start of season two?

10. How much money per week does Connor say he is spending on Willa's play?

Answers on page 91

ANSWERS

Answer Sheet: General Knowledge

1. Baseball/softball.

2. Kendall.

3. The family of the boy who didn't hit the home run from Roman's bet.

4. A stroke.

5. Greg.

6. Shiv.

7. Infidelities. She must have accidentally missed it out.

8. COO.

9. His personal trainer.

10. Nate. Lovely, no-ulterior-motive Nate.

Answer Sheet: General Knowledge

1. The annual foundation gala.

2. Connor.

3. On the company cruise ship.

4. Stewy.

5. Prostitute.

6. American Thanksgiving.

7. His medals. Much to Ewan's consternation.

8. Ewan and Tom.

9. He is dealing with an act of terrorism.

10. To impress a girl.

Answer Sheet: General Knowledge

1. Gerri and Stewy.

2. Kendall, Frank, Asha and Ilona. It does not go well for them.

3. Logan.

4. The satellite launch out of Japan.

5. Connor.

6. Greg.

7. An app to promote small artists.

8. Prague.

9. A club in an old railway bridge building.

10. Sandy Furness.

Answer Sheet: General Knowledge

1. Greg.

2. Connor.

3. Napoleonic history. There's considerable investment interest.

4. Caroline Collingwood.

5. President of the United States.

6. Nate.

7. Andrew Dodds.

8. Tom. Though "romantic" may be the wrong word.

9. The Hamptons.

10. A dead possum in the fireplace.

Answer Sheet: General Knowledge

1. Lobster.

2. His dad told him to.

3. Gerri and Karl.

4. Greg.

5. Frank.

6. Hungary.

7. Pigs.

8. Boar on the Floor.

9. Rat-f*cker Sam. Tom: "Is he nice? You're asking about the moral character of a man named rat-fucker Sam?"

10. Lester. Moe-Lester.

Answer Sheet: General Knowledge

1. A turkey.

2. Hitler's dog, Blondie. Mark spelled his dog's name differently, though.

3. "We're listening". Unfortunately it turned out that the company literally was listening.

4. Kendall, to Naomi Pierce.

5. "Secret".

6. Pigeon.

7. $120m or $20m plus the kids at her place every Christmas.

8. Helen.

9. 40%.

10. Jennifer.

Answer Sheet: General Knowledge

1. 50, in honor of Logan's 50th anniversary.

2. No Real Person Involved, meaning a cruise worker, dancer or someone else who doesn't matter.

3. Tom.

4. Karl and Jamie (Laird).

5. Eduard Asgarov.

6. Shiv.

7. Connor.

8. Gerri. Roman quickly and competently shuts that one down.

9. Tom. Alone, with Shiv or with Greg sprinkles as a party pack.

10. DJ Squiggle

Answer Sheet: Logan

1. His 80th.

2. Dundee, Scotland.

3. A helicopter.

4. Kendall's.

5. Iverson, Kendall's son.

6. Rose.

7. The Logan Roy School of Journalism. Ewan: "What's next, the Jack the Ripper Women's Health Clinic?"

8. Expansion into parks.

9. Hibernian.

10. That Connor drops his ill-advised bid for the US presidency. A good trade.

Answer Sheet: Kendall

1. Rava.

2. Iverson.

3. Two. The other is a daughter named Sophie.

4. Half a billion dollars.

5. Harvard.

6. Iceland.

7. Batteries, from a variety store.

8. Naomi Pierce.

9. "Awesome".

10. Greg.

Answer Sheet: Shiv

1. Roman.

2. Gil Eavis.

3. Chief of Staff.

4. His butt.

5. Connor.

6. Wikipedia.

7. "10 to 15 grand's worth". A typical birthday present budget, I'm sure you'll agree.

8. Eastmoor Castle.

9. CEO of Pierce Global Media (PGM) - Rhea's old job.

10. A scrapbook of the places they have lived.

Answer Sheet: Roman

1. Hit a home run in the family baseball game.

2. Romulus.

3. Dog food. Although it was apparently chocolate cake.

4. Shiv's wedding.

5. COO, or Chief Operating Officer.

6. Turkey.

7. Logan.

8. Hearts - aka Heart of Midlothian.

9. Tabitha.

10. Six weeks.

Answer Sheet: Connor

1. Sourdough starter. To make bread without yeast, the old school way. Of course, it goes down really well with Logan.

2. *Sand.*

3. Taxes.

4. Austerlitz.

5. "Connor Roy was interested in politics at a very young age."

6. $3,000. Only for the guy to shoot the dog in the car park.

7. Napoleon's penis.

8. Monopoly.

9. Water. It is for this reason that he has a giant aquifer under all of his farms which he owns the pumping rights to.

10. "I super-love you, superdad."

Answer Sheet: Tom

1. A watch. (A Patek Philippe watch, to be specific.)

2. Wambsgans.

3. Minnesota. His mother was a renowned lawyer/Garda as in the Twin Cities.

4. Greg.

5. "You Can't Make a Tomlet Without Breaking Some Gregs".

6. Roman. For some reason.

7. Chair of Global Broadcast News at ATN.

8. His chicken. Logan: "What's next? Stick his cock into my potato salad?"

9. Their non-existent dog.

10. Bill Lockheart.

Answer Sheet: Greg

1. Hirsch.

2. A dog.

3. "Greg the Egg". Apparently because he was shaped like an egg.

4. Gregory. Though no one appears to actually do this.

5. "Benign fungus."

6. Champagne.

7. Kendall, on the condition that he can party there, seemingly endlessly.

8. $250 million.

9. Bill Gates.

10. Foot fungus.

Answer Sheet: Marcia

1. Lebanon.

2. Shiv.

3. Turn off the music that's annoying him.

4. Amir.

5. Paris.

6. Publishing assistant.

7. Logan's pajamas and slippers.

8. Rhea.

9. Ewan.

10. True. Marcia has 343 compared to Willa's 292.

Answer Sheet: Gerri

1. Kellman.

2. General Counsel.

3. Baird.

4. 30 years ago. (Technically it's "over 30 years".)

5. Japan.

6. Shiv. Aren't you glad it's not Roman?

7. $3 billion.

8. COO.

9. Slime.

10. False. Gerri has 537 to Connor's 792.

Answer Sheet: Insults

1. "An unshaven candle." Kendall.

2. "A competent kind of clever filing cabinet." Gerri.

3. "Like a sex robot for Dad to f*ck." Kendall.

4. "Kim Jong Pop." Logan.

5. "Calamari c*ck-ring." Kendall. Kendall receives quite a lot of insults.

6. "Dildo dipped in beard trimmings." Stewy.

7. "Little Machiavellian f*ck." Greg.

8. "Honey badger." Shiv.

9. "The c*nt of Monte Cristo." Tom.

10. "F*cking Californian shrunken little raisin." The President of the United States. As described by Logan Roy.

Answer Sheet: Complete the Quote

1. Stone-cold killer bitch.

2. Butter. There were dinner rolls ripping out there as he spoke.

3. Sprinkles.

4. Marriott.

5. Can opener.

6. Grandpa Grumps.

7. Being too short.

8. Bulletproof Monk.

9. Meth head.

10. Dog getting f*cked on roller skates.

Answer Sheet: Connor's Heartfelt Eulogy

1. Human.

2. Man.

3. Employee.

4. Forty.

5. Sad.

6. Seventy-eight.

7. Wife.

8. Maria.

9. Fifteen.

10. Sad.

Answer Sheet: Complete the Quote

1. Bad plus terrible.

2. Thumbs.

3. Hyena farm.

4. Party.

5. Date rape.

6. Kittens and perverts.

7. 'Clining.

8. Rockstar and the mole woman.

9. Armani.

10. Hate speech.

Answer Sheet: Who Am I?

1. Greg.

2. Roman.

3. Tom.

4. Caroline.

5. Connor.

6. Rhea.

7. Logan.

8. Willa.

9. Shiv.

10. Kendall.

Answer Sheet: Anagrams

1. Brainy Oohs = Siobhan Roy.

2. Canine Rep = Nan Pierce.

3. Darkly Lone = Kendall Roy.

4. Mambo Twangs = Tom Wambsgans.

5. Loan Orgy = Logan Roy.

6. Corny Or No = Connor Roy.

7. Hoggish Cryerr = Gregory Hirsch.

8. Milk Enlarger = Gerri Kellman.

9. No Armory = Roman Roy.

10. A Minor Piece = Naomi Pierce.

Answer Sheet: Who Said It?

1. Kendall.

2. Roman.

3. Marcia. To Rhea. Badass.

4. Connor.

5. Tom.

6. Marcia.

7. Rhea.

8. Connor.

9. Kendall.

10. Greg.

Answer Sheet: In Real Life

1. Will Ferrell.

2. Sarah Snook, who plays Shiv.

3. *The Gentlemen.*

4. Jean.

5. Quebec.

6. *Speed.*

7. Fuller McCallister.

8. Mr. Darcy. Absolute dreamboat.

9. Holly Hunter, who plays Rhea. She won Best Actress in 1993 for her role as Ada McGrath in *The Piano.*

10. Australian.

Answer Sheet: Kendall's Rap

1. North Bank.

2. Sick ride.

3. Loot.

4. Fatty.

5. Hamptons time.

6. Wine.

7. Father Time.

8. Stan.

9. News.

10. Ring.

Answer Sheet: Cast & Crew

1. Jesse Armstrong.

2. Brian Cox.

3. Sarah Snook.

4. Matthew Macfadyen.

5. Jeremy Strong.

6. Kieran Culkin.

7. Adam McKay.

8. Nicholas Braun.

9. Alan Ruck.

10. J. Smith-Cameron.

Answer Sheet: Tiebreakers

1. 2018.

2. 130.

3. 3%.

4. $2m.

5. $5 million. "Can't retire. Not worth it to work. Oh, yes, five will drive you un poco loco."

6. 6 feet, 6 inches.

7. Four - Outstanding Drama Series, Outstanding Lead Actor in a Drama Series (Jeremy Strong), Outstanding Directing for a Drama Series (Android Parekh for "Hunting") and Outstanding Writing for a Drama Series (Jesse Armstrong for "This Is Not For Tears").

8. 10 years.

9. 48 hours.

10. How much money per week does Connor say he is spending on Willa's play? $500k.

Thanks for playing, quizzer! If you've enjoyed the book, please leave a review on Amazon: it only takes a minute and it really helps! Take care.

- Alex.

OTHER BOOKS BY ALEX MITCHELL

Quizzin' Nine-Nine: A Brooklyn Nine-Nine Quiz Book
Parks & Interrogation: A Parks & Recreation Quiz Book
Q & AC-12: A Line of Duty Quiz Book
Know Your Schitt: A Schitt's Creek Quiz Book
Examilton: A Hamilton Quiz Book
Stranger Thinks: A Stranger things Quiz Book
The El Clued Brothers: A Peep Show Quiz Book
Dunder Quizlin: An Office US Quiz Book

Printed in Great Britain
by Amazon